Who Is
Barack Obama?

Who Is
Barack Obama?

by Roberta Edwards

illustrated by John O'Brien

Penguin Workshop
An Imprint of Penguin Random House

For Tess—JO

PENGUIN WORKSHOP
Penguin Young Readers Group
An Imprint of Penguin Random House LLC

Library of Congress Control Number: 2009019369

ISBN 9780448453309

27 26 25

Contents

Who Is
Barack Obama?

There once was a young man who was a student at Columbia University. He had never lived in New York City before. It was 1981 and, for a year, he spent his free time walking all around the city. He was not only interested in seeing famous sights like the Statue of Liberty that many tourists visited, but he also wanted to visit other parts of the city, like Harlem. Harlem is a famous neighborhood where many black families have lived since the 1920s. The young man visited historic churches and the Apollo Theater. He heard Jesse Jackson, the civil rights leader, give a speech.

On his long walks, the young man kept
looking at people. He hoped to find where he fit
in. The young man's name was Barack Obama.
Tall and skinny with an Afro, he was half white
and half black. Often he felt he didn't belong
anywhere. He was unsure of his future. What
would he make of his life?

Back in 1981, if someone had said, "Guess who will be president of the United States in less than thirty years," Barack would never have said, "Me."

Yet on January 20, 2009, that is exactly what happened. Barack Hussein Obama was sworn in as the 44th president.

Imagine how surprised that college kid would be to find himself living in the White House!

Chapter 1
Born in Paradise

Hawaii is a group of islands that lie in the Pacific Ocean. Hawaii became a state in 1959, the same year as Alaska. The closest state to Hawaii is California, but they are more than two thousand miles apart.

The weather in Hawaii is beautiful all year long. Tropical flowers make the air smell sweet. There are palm trees and beautiful beaches. Even in the early morning, surfers are out riding the waves. They go surfing before school starts.

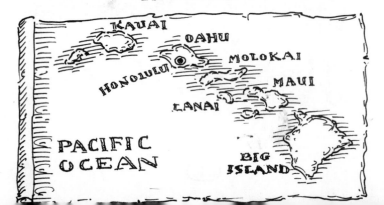

Honolulu is the capital of Hawaii. This is where
Barack Obama was born on August 4, 1961.

Barack's first name means "blessed" in Swahili,
an African language. Barack was his father's name,
too. But neither of the baby's parents called him
Barack. He was always "Barry."

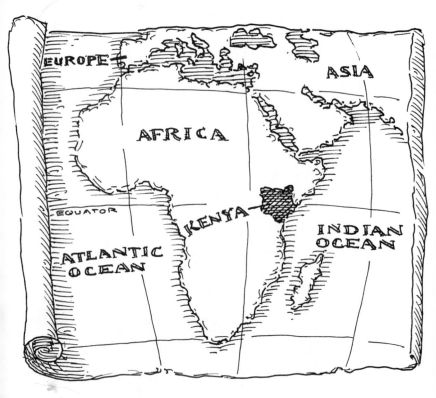

Barry's father was from Kenya, a country in Africa. He had come to Hawaii to study at the University of Hawaii. He met an eighteen-year-old girl who was a student there, too. She lived in Honolulu with her parents. Her name was Stanley Ann Dunham.

Why Stanley?

Stanley was her father's name. He had wanted a boy. So he named his only child, Stanley. But she was known as Ann to her friends.

Ann and Barack met, fell in love, and got married. There is nothing unusual about that except this happened in 1961. Ann was white; Barack was black. Back then, very few people of different races decided to marry each other. In fact, in some states, it was illegal!

Ann's parents were fairly open-minded people. They accepted their new son-in-law. He was smart and interesting. And they adored their chubby baby grandson. Little Barry grew up calling them Gramps and Toot. (In Hawaiian, "tutu" means grandmother.)

In Hawaii, many people have brown skin, so
Barry didn't look or feel any different. At the
beach, Gramps liked to fool tourists by saying
Barry was the great-grandson of a famous
Hawaiian king!

When Barry was two years old, his parents split up. His father wanted to study at Harvard University in Massachusetts. That was more than 5,000 miles away from Hawaii. Eventually Barack wanted to return to Kenya with Ann and Barry. But Ann did not want to live in a small village in Africa. So she stayed in Hawaii with her young son.

Barry was ten years old before he saw his father again. He had photos of Barack as well as the stories that his mom and grandparents told him about his father. But it wasn't enough. Barry felt as if there was a big hole in his heart.

Chapter 2
Lolo and Maya

In 1967, Barry's mother married a man named Lolo Soetoro. (In Hawaiian slang, the word "lolo" means crazy—Gramps thought that was a riot.) Lolo came from Indonesia, a country in the Pacific made up of many islands. Lolo had been studying at the University of Hawaii. That's where he and Ann met.

Little Barry liked Lolo right away. When Lolo returned to Indonesia, Ann and Barry went, too. Ann was ready to move away from her parents and become more independent.

INDONESIA

MORE THAN 17,000 ISLANDS IN THE PACIFIC AND INDIAN OCEANS MAKE UP THE COUNTRY OF INDONESIA. ONLY ABOUT SIX THOUSAND OF THESE ISLANDS HAVE PEOPLE LIVING ON THEM. THE CLIMATE IS TROPICAL WITH WET SEASONS. EXCEPT FOR BRAZIL, INDONESIA HAS A WIDER VARIETY OF ANIMALS AND PLANTS THAN ANY COUNTRY IN THE WORLD.

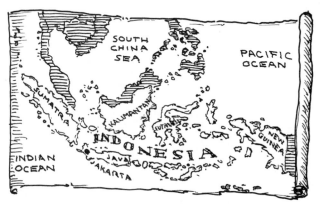

THERE ARE A LOT OF PEOPLE, TOO—ABOUT 240 MILLION. THE MAJORITY ARE MUSLIMS. THEY FOLLOW THE ISLAMIC RELIGION.

FOR MORE THAN THREE HUNDRED YEARS, THE DUTCH RULED THE AREA. BUT IN 1949, INDONESIA WON INDEPENDENCE. THAT, HOWEVER, DID NOT BRING DEMOCRACY. IT WAS NOT UNTIL 2004 THAT INDONESIA HELD ITS FIRST REAL ELECTION FOR PRESIDENT.

Living in Jakarta, the capital of Indonesia, was a great adventure for a six-year-old boy. Lolo got Barry a pet. Was it a puppy or a kitten? No! Lolo got Barry a little ape named Tata. Tata loved to swing from the branches in the trees above their house. Chickens and ducks lived in the yard— alligators, too!

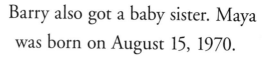

Barry also got a baby sister. Maya was born on August 15, 1970.

Barry went to a local public school for two years and then to a Catholic school. In both first grade and third grade, he wrote that he wanted to be president when he grew up. Many kids say that, but in Barry's case, it really came true! Today, tour buses stop at the schools where he went and pass the small house where his family lived.

Barry's mother was now a teacher. Lolo was a businessman. He was a good stepfather. He thought of Barry as his own son. When an older boy picked on Barry, Lolo bought two pairs of boxing gloves, a big pair for himself and a little pair for Barry.

He wanted to make sure Barry could stand up
for himself. So he taught him how to box.

Ann was concerned that Barry might fall behind in English. So every day, she woke him up at four o'clock in the morning to give him English lessons before school. Barry would try anything he could to get out of his lessons. But Ann never listened to excuses. She told Barry, "This is no picnic for me either, Buster."

She also taught him American history. Most of all, she wanted him to know about the black civil rights movement.

Even though Barry lived thousands of miles away, he was still a United States citizen. He needed to be aware of the great changes taking place in his country. She told him about civil rights leaders, like Martin Luther King, Jr.

MARTIN LUTHER KING, JR.

What exactly are civil rights?

The right to vote is one. So is the right to a decent education and a decent job.

For a long time, in the United States, African Americans were denied these basic rights. But in the 1960s, new laws were passed to provide equal rights to black people.

The Civil Rights Act was passed in 1964; the Voting Rights Law in 1965. Because of his mother, nine-year-old Barry began to understand what being black meant in the United States.

JIM CROW LAWS

THE END OF THE CIVIL WAR ALSO BROUGHT AN END TO SLAVERY. HOWEVER, UNTIL THE MIDDLE OF THE 20TH CENTURY, BLACK PEOPLE WERE OFTEN TREATED AS SECOND-CLASS CITIZENS. THIS WAS MOST TRUE IN SOME SOUTHERN STATES. BLACK PEOPLE WERE KEPT APART FROM WHITE PEOPLE THROUGH LAWS KNOWN AS JIM CROW LAWS. (THE NAME MAY HAVE COME FROM A BLACK CHARACTER IN SONG-AND-DANCE SHOWS POPULAR IN THE 1800S.)

BLACK PEOPLE COULD NOT EAT IN THE SAME RESTAURANTS OR STAY IN THE SAME HOTELS AS WHITE PEOPLE. SIGNS IN STORE WINDOWS SAID:

"FOR WHITES ONLY." BLACK FAMILIES COULD NOT BUY HOMES IN A WHITE NEIGHBORHOOD; BLACK CHILDREN COULD NOT GO TO THE SAME SCHOOL AS WHITE CHILDREN. THERE WERE EVEN SEPARATE WATER FOUNTAINS, SEPARATE SEATING AREAS IN MOVIE THEATERS AND BASEBALL PARKS, AND SEPARATE SEATS ON BUSES.

THE IDEA WAS THAT THE TWO RACES WOULD BE "SEPARATE, BUT EQUAL." ONLY THE SYSTEM WAS NEVER EQUAL—A WATER FOUNTAIN FOR BLACK PEOPLE WOULD BARELY WORK, WHILE THE ONE NEXT TO IT FOR WHITES WOULD BE LOVELY AND MODERN.

Chapter 3
Back to Hawaii

The longer the family stayed in Jakarta, the more Ann worried about her son. Barry was bright. He belonged at a better school.

With help from Gramps's boss, Barry won a place at a top private school in Hawaii—the Punahou School. So Ann sent Barry back—alone—to live with his grandparents. Barry had never been separated from his mother before. He was only ten.

PUNAHOU SCHOOL

His first day at the new school was every kid's nightmare. He felt like a freak. The other kids laughed at him. Barack Obama—what kind of name was that? His clothes weren't right. He wasn't rich like most of the kids. And there was only one other black student—a girl—in his class.

Barry tried his best to fit in and find friends. Mostly he tried not to stick out too much.

On top of everything he was dealing with at school, Barry also found out that his father was coming to visit. Barry had not seen him in eight years. What did he remember? Not much. The stories his mother told made his father sound strong and heroic. Like an African prince.

Yet the man he met was very thin, had a small beard, and wore thick glasses. Because of a bad car accident, he walked with a cane. The elder Barack Obama was nothing like what his son had imagined.

Barack Obama, Sr., remained in Hawaii for one month. Ann was in Hawaii for this family reunion, too. Barry's father stayed with Toot and Gramps. It was not an easy time for Barry. One day after his homework was done, Barry went to watch TV. But his dad said Barry should read instead because TV was a waste of time. Oh, how Barry resented being told what to do! What right did his dad have to suddenly show up and order him around?

His father also planned to come to Barry's new school and speak to his class. He was going to talk about life in Kenya. Many years later, Barry wrote, "I couldn't imagine anything worse." What would everybody think of his dad?

But the kids loved hearing about Africa. They were fascinated by the mud huts in his father's tiny village in Kenya. And they were amazed that, in Kenya, animals like elephants, lions, buffalo, and hippos lived in the wild, not in zoos.

At the end of Barack, Sr.'s talk, everyone

clapped. One boy told Barry that his dad was "cool." But actually Barry didn't need to be told. He saw that for himself.

After that day, Barry got along much better with his father. In the afternoons, they'd sit together and read. His father taught him how

to dance in the African style. His dad had a limp but he still could move!

After their month together, Barack Sr. returned to Kenya. Barry did not know it at the time, but he would never see his father again.

Chapter 4
Growing Up

By the time he was a teenager, Barry had settled into life at Punahou. Kids liked him and he was on the basketball team. That meant a lot to him. Not just because it was fun to play a game at which he was good. Being part of a group made him feel like he belonged. His nickname was Barry O'Bomber because of his great jump shot.

His mom was no longer married to Lolo, and she and Maya returned to Hawaii. Ann found a small apartment and Barry moved in, too.

After three years, Ann decided to move again —back to Jakarta. Ann was studying for a PhD in anthropology. (Anthropology is the study of different cultures.) She needed to return to

Indonesia to write about the life of rural women living there. She wanted Barry to go back, too. There was a good American school now in Jakarta.

But Barry said no. He wanted to stay in Hawaii. So he moved back in with Toot and Gramps. In June 1979, he graduated from Punahou. That fall, he started college at Occidental, a small, coed school near Pasadena, California. For the first time in his life, Barry was living on the mainland of the United States.

Barry had never worked very hard in high school. He was very smart, but he didn't push himself to be a top student. However, he did love to read. Like his mother, he was interested in American history—especially black history. He read books by famous black writers like Langston Hughes and Richard Wright. He also read about the life of Malcolm X. Most civil rights leaders, like Martin Luther King, Jr., wanted blacks and whites to live together as equals. Not Malcolm X. He believed blacks would grow stronger by separating

themselves from white people.

As for Barry Obama, he was trying to figure out what made sense to him.

MARTIN LUTHER KING, JR., AND MALCOLM X

MARTIN LUTHER KING, JR., AND MALCOLM X BOTH WANTED WHITE PEOPLE TO STOP PUTTING DOWN, OR OPPRESSING, BLACK PEOPLE. BUT THEY DID NOT AGREE ON WHAT WOULD MAKE THIS HAPPEN.

MARTIN LUTHER KING, JR., WAS BORN IN GEORGIA IN 1929. HE WAS A MINISTER. WORDS WERE HIS WEAPON. HE USED WORDS TO ENCOURAGE PEOPLE TO STAND UP FOR WHAT WAS RIGHT. HE BELIEVED THAT PEACEFUL PROTESTS—LIKE MARCHES, RALLIES, AND SIT-INS—WOULD EVENTUALLY MAKE WHITE PEOPLE ACCEPT BLACKS AS EQUALS. IN APRIL 1968, MARTIN LUTHER KING, JR., WAS SHOT AND KILLED IN MEMPHIS, TENNESSEE. HE WAS ONLY THIRTY-NINE YEARS OLD.

MARTIN LUTHER KING, JR.

MALCOLM X

MALCOLM LITTLE WAS BORN IN OMAHA, NEBRASKA, ON MAY 19, 1925. MALCOLM WAS SMART, BUT DROPPED OUT OF SCHOOL AND BEGAN GETTING INTO TROUBLE. HE SPENT SEVEN YEARS IN JAIL FOR ROBBERY. IN JAIL, HE TURNED HIS LIFE AROUND. HE TOOK A NEW NAME—MALCOLM X. (HE THOUGHT LITTLE WAS A "SLAVE NAME.") HE JOINED THE NATION OF ISLAM, A GROUP THAT WANTED A SEPARATE STATE FOR BLACK PEOPLE. A POWERFUL SPEAKER, MALCOLM X THOUGHT THAT SOMETIMES VIOLENCE WAS THE ONLY WAY TO MAKE CHANGE HAPPEN. HOWEVER, TOWARD THE END OF HIS LIFE, HIS VIEWS WERE CHANGING, MOVING CLOSER TO THOSE OF MARTIN LUTHER KING, JR., THEN, ON FEBRUARY 21, 1965, HE WAS SHOT AND KILLED IN NEW YORK CITY BY THREE MEN IN THE NATION OF ISLAM.

LIKE MARTIN LUTHER KING, JR., MALCOLM X WAS ALSO THIRTY-NINE YEARS OLD WHEN HE DIED.

At Oxy, the nickname for the college, Barry hung out with other black students. They talked a lot about politics. He became interested in South Africa. In that country, black people were kept completely apart from whites under a terrible system known as apartheid. (It wasn't until 1994 that South Africa held elections where people of all races could vote.)

Barry invited speakers to come talk about South Africa. He decided to speak up about apartheid, too. In his first speech, he noticed that the audience was really listening to him. He liked seeing the power of his words.

For the first time, he began calling himself Barack. Partly because a beautiful, older girl told him it was a great name. But also because he now felt that it was a great name, too, a name that belonged to him.

Chapter 5
City Life

After two years at Oxy, Barack transferred to Columbia University. Its campus is on the Upper West Side of Manhattan, close to Harlem. On his

COLUMBIA UNIVERSITY

walks around the city, Barack saw other black neighborhoods. He saw families living in terrible poverty—right here in America, not South Africa.

Barack worked hard at Columbia. He also ran three miles a day. He kept a diary of his thoughts and experiences. He was becoming a more serious, mature person.

In the summer, Barack worked at a construction site. His mother and sister came to New York for a long visit. They'd spend evenings with Barack.

A letter had come from Barack's father. For
several years, the two had hardly been in touch.
However, in this letter, the elder Obama asked his
son to visit him. Barack agreed to go to Kenya
after graduation. It was a chance to get to know
his father better.

When Barack told Ann about his plans, she was thrilled. She hoped the two men could become close. But in 1982 (one year before Barack graduated), Barack Obama, Sr., died in a car accident. He was only forty-six years old.

Losing a parent is always hard, no matter how old a child is. The death of his father made Barack take life more seriously. He gave more thought to his future. What did he want to do after college? How could he make a difference in the world? He needed to make enough money to pay off student loans. But after that, he wanted to help black communities. He hoped to make poor people's lives better.

After graduating from Columbia, Barack moved to Chicago, Illinois. He became a community organizer. His job was to work directly with poor people to fix problems. What kinds of problems? Maybe a landlord in an apartment wasn't giving proper heat to tenants.

Maybe gangs were making people afraid to leave their homes. Maybe a neighborhood needed a training program for people without jobs.

One time a young mother came to see Barack. She lived in an apartment building that offered low rents for poor families. The building was not well kept. Worse, she worried that there might be asbestos in the walls of her apartment. (Asbestos was used to construct buildings until it was found to be harmful to our lungs.) The landlord said tests had been done and there was no asbestos in the apartments. However, when the young woman asked to see the test results, no copy could be found.

Barack organized a group that included the young woman and other mothers with small children. They went to the landlord's office and found that, indeed, no tests for asbestos had ever been done. The landlord was afraid that there would be newspaper stories about him. So he started tests that day. The result? There was asbestos, and the building got emergency cleanup money.

It was satisfying to see change happen. However, the more time he spent in Chicago, the more Barack believed the best way to change the lives of the poor was through the law. Lawyers can bring cases to court; lawyers get to know people in power; lawyers can even work to pass new laws.

To be a lawyer, Barack needed to go to law school. So he applied to Harvard Law School in Boston, Massachusetts. Harvard is one of the greatest law schools in the United States. Barack was accepted!

AUSTIN HALL, HARVARD

But before classes started in the fall, there was a trip he had to take. The trip had been on his mind for many years.

That July, he flew to Kenya. In Africa, Barack would finally meet his father's family. Barack had many half brothers and half sisters. Now they would become more than simply names to him.

Chapter 6
Coming Home

When Barack got off the plane in Kenya, his
suitcase was lost. It wasn't a good start to the trip.

But then something nice happened. The bag handler heard Barack's name, and asked if he was related to the famous Dr. Barack Obama. Barack felt so proud. Kenya is a fairly big country, yet his father's name was well-known and respected.

The Obamas came from a small village called Kogelo in the western part of the country. Some people there still lived in huts. Barack stayed in

the apartment of one of his half sisters. Her name was Auma. Outside in her yard, monkeys played. But they weren't pets like Tata. These monkeys were free!

Kenya was not like any place Barack had ever

seen. In parks, at the marketplace, and in stores, most people were black. Yes, he'd see some white people, but only a small number. At last, Barack did not feel like an outsider. When he first met one of his aunts, she said, "Welcome home."

There was a party for Barack. He met more relatives. (Over the years, Barack's father had had four wives, so there were lots of relatives.) It

turned out that his half brother Bernard was as crazy about basketball as Barack was.

Barack met his grandmother. She told him

stories about his father that Barack's mother had no way of knowing. Granny described his father as a child—smart, restless, and eager to make the most of his life.

In her backyard were the graves of both his father and grandfather. When Barack kneeled down to pay his respects, he cried. There are good kinds of crying and bad kinds of crying. This was the good kind.

By the time he left two weeks later, Barack really felt as though he was part of the family.

As for the people in Kenya, they too felt that Barack Obama was now part of their family. On Election Day 2008, American flags flew all across the country. When the news came that Obama had won, people poured out of their houses, singing, dancing, and waving posters of

Obama. Barack's grandmother threw a big outdoor party for everyone in the village. There was a feast with beef, lamb, and goat, which is considered very special.

A public holiday was declared for the whole country two days later. Although not born in Kenya, Barack Obama is thought of as a native son.

KENYA

KENYA, WHOSE CAPITAL IS NAIROBI, IS IN EAST AFRICA. IT SITS RIGHT ON THE EQUATOR. MOST PEOPLE THERE SPEAK BOTH ENGLISH AND SWAHILI. LIKE THE UNITED STATES, KENYA HAS AN ELECTED PRESIDENT AND SEPARATE BRANCHES OF GOVERNMENT. KENYA BECAME AN INDEPENDENT COUNTRY IN 1963. (THE BRITISH RULED THE AREA UNTIL THEN.)

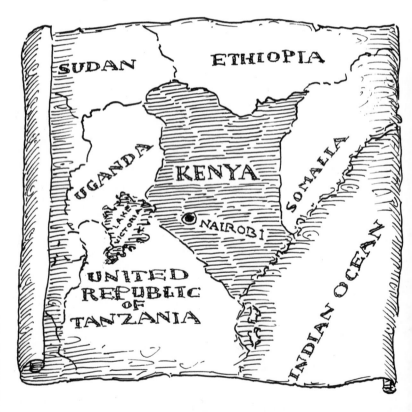

AFTER INDEPENDENCE, MANY OF THE BEST JOBS IN GOVERNMENT WENT TO PEOPLE IN THE KIKUKU TRIBE (THE LARGEST TRIBE IN KENYA). THE OBAMAS WERE FROM THE LUO TRIBE. BARACK'S FATHER SPOKE OUT, SAYING THE BEST JOBS SHOULD GO TO THE BEST PEOPLE—NO MATTER WHAT TRIBE THEY WERE FROM. THE NEW PRESIDENT, JOMO KENYATTA, DID NOT LIKE THIS. HE SAW TO IT THAT BARACK'S FATHER HAD TROUBLE FINDING ANY JOB IN KENYA. ALL THIS HAPPENED IN THE YEARS BEFORE HE VISITED YOUNG BARRY IN HAWAII.

Chapter 7
Michelle

Even among all the smart students at Harvard Law, Barack Obama stood out. At twenty-seven, he was older than the other students and more mature. In class, he wasn't only interested in answering questions. He liked listening to other people's opinions.

It takes three years to earn a law degree. After his first year, Barack returned to Chicago for the summer. He was hired at a big law firm. He couldn't show up in jeans and sneakers. So Barack had to go out and buy new clothes.

For a summer job, the pay was very good. Still
Barack did not plan to work at a firm like this
after law school. He held onto his dream of
helping the poor.

A beautiful young woman showed him around
the offices on his first day. Her name was
Michelle Robinson. She had lived in Chicago all
her life. Even though she was two years younger
than Barack, she was already a lawyer. That was

because Michelle had gone straight to law school after college. (She, too, went to Harvard Law.)

They had lunch together the first day. Right away Barack was drawn to Michelle. She was so smart and striking-looking. Almost six feet tall, Michelle was only a couple of inches shorter than Barack. She had a quick sense of humor and she

wasn't shy about telling people exactly what was on her mind.

But Michelle was only interested in being friends . . . or so she said. She thought dating anyone at the law firm was "tacky."

Even so, by the time he returned to Harvard, Barack and Michelle had fallen in love. The romance continued long-distance while Barack finished law school.

During his last year at law school, Barack was elected president of the *Harvard Law Review*. The *Harvard Law Review* is a magazine with articles

on important questions of law. The president is the top editor. It was a very big honor. And because Barack was the first African American

ever chosen, newspapers ran stories about him. Then, an editor saw the stories and asked him to write a book. Barack's book, *Dreams from My Father*, came out in 1995. In it, Barack talks about growing up without a father and being raised by his white relatives. The book describes his struggle to find a place for himself in the world. It is beautifully written. If Barack had not chosen a life in politics, he might have become a famous writer.

Chapter 8
Putting Down Roots

In 1991, after law school, Barack returned to
Chicago and Michelle. They were married the
following year. He took a job at a law firm.

The firm handled many civil rights cases.
He also taught evening classes at the University

of Chicago Law School. His class was about the
Constitution.

THE CONSTITUTION

IN 1783, THE AMERICAN COLONIES WON THE WAR FOR INDEPENDENCE. NOW THE NEW COUNTRY, THE UNITED STATES OF AMERICA, NEEDED TO DECIDE WHAT KIND OF GOVERNMENT WOULD WORK BEST.

FOUR YEARS LATER, THE CONSTITUTION WAS WRITTEN AT A CONVENTION IN PHILADELPHIA. GEORGE WASHINGTON WAS HEAD OF THE CONVENTION. IT MAPPED OUT A GOVERNMENT WITH THREE BRANCHES OF POWER—A STRONG PRESIDENT, A CONGRESS TO PASS LAWS, AND COURTS TO DECIDE WHETHER THE LAWS WERE FAIR. THE PRESIDENT AND MEMBERS OF CONGRESS WOULD BE ELECTED. THE TOP JUDGES, HOWEVER, WERE TO BE CHOSEN BY THE PRESIDENT.

ALTHOUGH THE CONSTITUTION IS NOW MORE

THAN TWO HUNDRED YEARS OLD, IT IS AS IMPORTANT TODAY AS EVER. DIFFERENT MEANINGS CAN BE READ FROM SOME OF ITS WORDS. FOR A LONG TIME, THE SUPREME COURT RULED THAT SEGREGATION WAS LEGAL BECAUSE THE CONSTITUTION DID NOT FORBID IT. (THE CONSTITUTION DID NOT OUTLAW SLAVERY EITHER.) THEN, IN 1954, A CIVIL RIGHTS CASE WAS BROUGHT BEFORE THE SUPREME COURT. THE JUDGES DECIDED THAT SCHOOLS COULD NOT BE SEGREGATED, AND THAT SEPARATE WAS NEVER EQUAL. IN TEACHING HIS CLASS, BARACK OBAMA AND HIS STUDENTS WOULD HAVE ARGUED ABOUT THE MEANING OF VARIOUS PARTS OF THE CONSTITUTION. SOME DISCUSSIONS MIGHT EVEN HAVE BEEN ABOUT THE POWERS OF THE PRESIDENT.

As Michelle's husband, Barack was now part of a strong, close family. The Robinsons had deep roots in Chicago. Michelle's parents still lived there. So did her older brother, Craig. When Michelle was a child, her parents' idea of fun on a Saturday night was to stay home and play board games with their kids. Barack had always wanted to grow up in a family like that.

His own family was going through a very difficult time. Gramps had died and his mother was suffering from cancer. She moved back to Hawaii to be near Toot. Ann died on November 7, 1995. Barack was not with her. To this day, he says that remains the biggest regret of his life.

Why did he stay in Chicago? Because he had just begun his very first campaign for public office.

Just as the United States Congress passes laws that affect the whole country, each state has a government that passes state laws. In 1995, Barack decided to run for one of the state Senate seats in Illinois.

Barack was a Democrat. He was running in an area where most voters were Democrats and also black. He won the election by many votes. Barack was thirty-five years old. It was the start of his political career.

State governments work in the state capitals. The capital of Illinois is Springfield, a city about one hundred and seventy-five miles from Chicago.

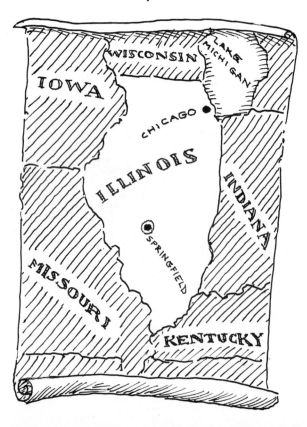

As a state senator, Barack had to spend part of
every week in Springfield. That meant being away
from Michelle whose job kept her in Chicago. It
was lonely for them both. After their daughter
Malia was born in 1998, being apart became
twice as hard. (Malia means "calm" in Hawaiian
and "queen" in Swahili.)

Michelle was now working for the University of Chicago. With Barack often gone, the care of the baby fell on her and her alone. Her own mother had been a stay-at-home mom when Michelle and her brother were children. But that was in the 1960s when only about 30 percent of women with young children had full-time jobs. Now it was the 1990s. Almost 70 percent of mothers of young children worked full time. Like most people, the Obamas depended on two salaries to make a decent life for their family.

Although he felt guilty about being away, Barack found his work fascinating. Different parts of the state had such different problems and needs. Most of the members in the Illinois Senate, besides being white and Republican, represented districts where many voters were farmers. State

senators from these areas might, for example, push for tax breaks on farmland. Barack, on the other hand, represented people who lived in a huge city. They needed more jobs, better housing, and safer neighborhoods.

Barack really enjoyed the give and take of working in the Senate. He was good at reaching agreements and knowing when to compromise. He was able to get laws passed to help the people in his Chicago district. These included laws to create after-school programs, remove dangerous lead from homes, and limit how politicians raise money.

Barack was ambitious, and he was also impatient. He was in a hurry to get ahead. If he hadn't realized that before, he certainly knew it now. Staying in the state senate forever was not his dream. He thought about running for mayor of Chicago. But instead, he decided to run for a seat in the US House of Representatives in 2000.

The district was in Chicago where most voters
were black Democrats. However, the current
congressman was a famous civil rights leader.
Next to him, Barack seemed too young and too
unknown. Barack lost and lost big—by thirty
percentage points.

So he returned to work in Springfield. He
remained a state senator until 2005.

Chapter 9
A Growing Family

In 2001, Malia became a big sister. On June 10, Barack and Michelle's second daughter, Natasha (Sasha for short), was born.

Michelle and Barack settled into their life as working parents of young children. Michelle was on staff at the University of Chicago's hospitals. She was in charge of setting up health clinics for the poor. Her salary was much higher than Barack's. It helped pay off their loans from law school. Barack remained in the Illinois Senate. (He was so popular among voters that in the 2002 election, no one ran against him!)

Then, on September 11, 2001, the world changed suddenly for the Obamas, just as it did for everyone in America.

Terrorists flew planes into the World Trade Center in New York City and the Pentagon building in Washington, D.C. The terrorists belonged to a Muslim group called Al Qaeda.

In early 2002, the United States declared war in Afghanistan where Osama bin Laden, the leader of Al Qaeda, was thought to be hiding. A year later, the country went to war in Iraq.

Once again, Barack started thinking about running for a higher office. At such an important time, he wanted to be in Washington, helping to decide the questions of the day. For example, the US Congress had backed President George W. Bush in the decision to wage war against Iraq. The president claimed that Iraq had weapons that could destroy the United States.

GEORGE W. BUSH

Barack Obama, however, was not convinced that these weapons existed. (It turned out that, indeed, they didn't.) Barack thought finding Osama bin Laden was more important than starting a war in Iraq. Early on, he was one of the few politicians who spoke out against the war.

OSAMA BIN LADEN

Like all states, Illinois has two US senators. One of them, a Republican named Peter Fitzgerald, decided not to run again in the 2004 election. Barack wanted to win his Senate seat very badly. He spent two years planning his campaign.

Michelle was not eager for Barack to run. If Barack won, he would be working in Washington,

D.C. Either the family would have to move or Barack would be away from home even more. Yet she backed her husband in pursuit of his dream.

By the summer of 2004, it seemed very likely that Barack would win the Senate race. That same summer, both Republicans and Democrats were holding conventions to pick a candidate for president.

The Democrats asked Barack Obama to give an important speech, called the Keynote speech, at their convention in Boston. Usually someone famous is the Keynote speaker. But Barack was chosen. He was young, smart, African American, and an outspoken critic of President Bush. (President Bush was running for a second term.)

Barack's speech was seen by millions of people across the country. He talked about his dreams for himself and his dreams for America. Only in America, he said, could a skinny kid with a funny name be running for senator. His hope was for all Americans—Republican, Democrat, white, black, old, and young—to work together

to make our country stronger and better.

Overnight, Barack Obama became famous.

Chapter 10
Bigger Dreams

That November, Barack Obama won the
Senate election in Illinois. In more than one

hundred twenty-five years, only two other African Americans had been elected to the US Senate. Now, at forty-three, he was also among the youngest senators ever. He took office on January 4, 2005, with Michelle and both his daughters at his side.

But his family was not going to move from Chicago to Washington. Michelle still worked for the University of Chicago hospitals. The girls, now six and three, were busy with school and friends. Barack, once again, would live apart from his family for part of each week.

In the Senate, the newer senators have far less power than long-time senators. Yet Barack quickly began working on the issues that had been important to him for so long—fair housing, affordable health care, and better schools. Other Democrats saw him as a young man with a great future ahead of him.

Still, many people were surprised when only

two years later, in February 2007, Barack Obama
announced he was going to run for president. The
next election would be on November 4, 2008.

Yes, Barack was smart and hard-working. Yes,
he was a wonderful speaker. Yes, he had been an
early critic of the Iraq war. And, yes, more and
more Americans now agreed with him that the
war was a mistake. But he was forty-five. He had
only been serving in the US Senate for two years.

A lot of people had no idea who he was. They thought his name was Barack Yo-Mama or Barack Alabama. Those who had heard of him wondered if he was ready to lead the entire country. And, of course, there was the issue of race. The United States had never had a black president. Was there any chance that Barack Obama could win?

BLACK PRESIDENTIAL CANDIDATES

SHIRLEY CHISHOLM

BARACK OBAMA WAS NOT THE FIRST AFRICAN AMERICAN TO RUN FOR PRESIDENT. IN 1972, A US CONGRESSWOMAN FROM NEW YORK TRIED TO BECOME THE DEMOCRATIC CANDIDATE FOR PRESIDENT. HER NAME WAS SHIRLEY CHISHOLM.

IN 1984, AND AGAIN IN 1988, JESSE JACKSON, A FAMOUS CIVIL RIGHTS LEADER AND ALSO A DEMOCRAT, TRIED TO WIN THE NOMINATION. BUT BEFORE 2008 NEITHER MAJOR PARTY HAD EVER CHOSEN AN AFRICAN AMERICAN AS ITS CANDIDATE.

JESSE JACKSON

A POLITICIAN FROM ILLIONOIS

ABRAHAM LINCOLN, THE 16TH PRESIDENT, IS
ONE OF THE MOST FAMOUS NAMES IN AMERICAN
HISTORY. BUT THAT CERTAINLY
WASN'T TRUE WHEN HE RAN
FOR PRESIDENT IN 1860.

HE HAD SERVED ONLY
ONE TWO-YEAR TERM AS
A US CONGRESSMAN.
LIKE BARACK OBAMA,
ABRAHAM LINCOLN WAS
A LAWYER FROM
ILLINOIS. AND, LIKE
OBAMA, LINCOLN
BECAME FAMOUS AS A
POWERFUL SPEAKER.

ABRAHAM LINCOLN

LINCOLN TOOK
OFFICE RIGHT BEFORE

THE START OF THE CIVIL WAR. IT WAS ABRAHAM
LINCOLN WHO ENDED SLAVERY IN THE UNITED
STATES. IT WAS THE BEGINNING OF A NEW CHAPTER
IN THE HISTORY OF BLACK PEOPLE IN AMERICA.

In 2007, no one was sure who would be the Republican candidate for president. (George W. Bush could not run again because he had already served two full terms.)

As for the Democrats, many thought Hillary Clinton would be their party's candidate. The wife of former president Bill Clinton, Hillary Clinton was a senator from New York. She was famous—everyone knew who she was. She was also very smart and hard-working.

HILLARY AND BILL CLINTON

Barack and Hillary agreed on most issues. But she had voted with President Bush to go to war in Iraq. The war was unpopular and kept dragging on year after year. And Hillary Clinton was a woman—was the country ready for a female president?

In the first six months of 2008, the two met in debates that were broadcast on TV. They went from state to state, giving speeches to get voters behind them. State contests—known as primaries and caucuses—began in January 2008. By early June, it was clear that Barack Obama had the support of more Democrats than Hillary Clinton.

2008 DEMOCRATIC CONVENTION

Barack accepted the nomination at the Democratic convention in Denver. He spoke outdoors from Mile High Stadium to eighty thousand people. He said, "Government cannot solve all our problems but what it should do is that which we cannot do for ourselves—protect us from harm and provide every child with a decent education; keep our water clean and our toys safe; invest in new schools and new roads and new science and technology."

It was August 28, 2008. The date is important. Why? Exactly forty-five years earlier, Martin Luther King, Jr., had given his famous "I have a dream" speech at a huge civil rights rally in Washington, D.C.

JOHN McCAIN

Now the general election began. Barack's Republican opponent was John McCain. A longtime senator from Arizona, he was a Vietnam War hero who spent five years in a prisoner-of-war camp. At seventy-two, McCain was one of the oldest men to run for president. As for the war in Iraq, he still believed there could be a victory. He was against many of the government programs that Barack wanted to fund.

The two men and their running mates criss-crossed the country for several months. Some days, Barack would speak at three or four rallies, each in a different state. He did take a couple of

days off, however, to visit Toot. She was very sick and Barack needed to see his grandmother one last time. He was not going to make the same mistake he had made with his mother.

Over the summer, the sky-high prices of gasoline were on every voter's mind. Suddenly, that fall, the economy tanked. People could not afford to pay their mortgages. They were losing their homes. Banks no longer had money to give loans, so businesses closed. That meant people were out of jobs.

The Republicans had been in power since 2001. Maybe it was time for a change. In fact, that was Barack Obama's motto—"Change We Can Believe In."

On November 4, 2008, one hundred and twenty-five

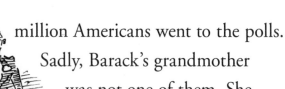

million Americans went to the polls.
Sadly, Barack's grandmother
was not one of them. She
died only two days before
the election.

The news was in before
midnight. Barack Obama would be the next
president of the United States. When he, Michelle,
and the girls greeted a crowd of one hundred and
twenty-five thousand people in a Chicago park,
he exclaimed, "What a scene, what a crowd . . .
Wow!"

Chapter 11
Change Has Come

"Change has come to America," Obama told the Chicago crowd on election night. The headline of the front page of the *New York Times* was only one word—and that word said it all: OBAMA.

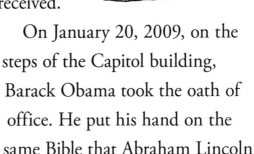

Almost sixty-seven million people voted for him, eight and a half million more votes than John McCain received.

On January 20, 2009, on the steps of the Capitol building, Barack Obama took the oath of office. He put his hand on the same Bible that Abraham Lincoln

had when he was sworn in as president. The crowds stretched for two miles to watch this moment in history. It was the largest crowd that had ever gathered in Washington, D.C.

That afternoon, the Obamas moved into the White House. It had been a long time since young children had lived in the mansion. Newspapers and magazines went wild over the new First Family. Michelle planted a vegetable garden. Michelle's mother also moved in to help care for the girls. So now the country had a First Grandma, too! But perhaps the biggest news of all was the arrival, in April 2009, of the girls' Portuguese water dog, Bo. A second Portuguese water dog, Sunny, joined the family in 2013.

PORTUGUESE
WATER DOG

No matter how big it is, any family can live very comfortably in the White House. It has 132 rooms. But Michelle wanted the girls' lives to stay as normal as possible. In fact, she told the staff not to make their beds or clean their rooms. That was *their* job.

Barack Obama jumped into his job as president. He picked his cabinet—the men and women who advise him on how to run the government. One of the most important cabinet posts is Secretary of State. For that, Obama picked Hillary Clinton. She was now in charge of dealing with other countries, especially war-torn areas like Iraq and the Middle East.

Barack Obama began his presidency at one of the most difficult times in the country's history. The economy was in danger of collapsing, and the United States was still at war in Iraq and in Afghanistan. Very quickly, Obama put forth plans to keep banks in business, to aid the auto industry, and to help people who were in danger of losing their homes. He also worked to pass a law that made health care affordable and available to all Americans. And by the end of 2011, he had pulled troops out of Iraq.

A president's days are long. The pressure is fierce. But Barack stayed true to his nickname. No Drama Obama always appeared calm, even as he ordered a team of US Navy SEALs to raid a

compound in Pakistan where Osama bin Laden, the man who was behind the terrorist attacks of September 11, was hiding. On the evening of May 1, 2011, President Obama announced to the country that bin Laden had been killed.

Despite many successes, Obama had more work to do. He asked the American people for their vote again in 2012. His Republican opponent was Mitt Romney, a businessman and the former governor of Massachusetts. On November 6, 2012, more than sixty-two million Americans voted to give Barack Obama four more years in the White House.

President Obama faced challenges in his second term. The economy was growing, but slowly. Republicans controlled Congress, and they would not pass many of the laws Obama proposed.

There were challenges overseas, too. A new terrorist group called ISIS had gained strength in Iraq. Obama sent troops back to Iraq to help fight the terrorists. He ordered airstrikes on the terrorists in the neighboring country of Syria.

Iran, another Middle East country, was close to building a nuclear weapon. Under Obama's leadership, the United States, along with five other nations, worked with Iran to curb their nuclear program.

In 2015, President Obama restored relations with the island nation of Cuba. The next year, he became the first US president since 1928 to visit the country. It was a historic occasion.

During Obama's eight years as president, the country added nearly ten million jobs. More than twenty million Americans gained health insurance. And the president took important steps to protect the environment.

"America is a better, stronger place than it was when we started," Obama said during his farewell speech in 2016. But he reminded the crowd: "Change only happens when ordinary people get involved, get engaged, and come together to demand it."

TIMELINE OF BARACK OBAMA'S LIFE

1961 — Barack Obama is born in Honolulu, Hawaii

1967 — Barack's mother remarries, and Barack moves with his mother and stepfather to Jakarta, Indonesia

1971 — Barack returns to Hawaii and lives with his grandparents
Barack's father comes from Africa for a visit

1983 — Barack graduates from Columbia University

1985 — Barack becomes a community organizer in Chicago, Illinoi

1988 — Barack visits his father's family in Kenya
Barack meets Michelle Robinson

1991 — Barack graduates from Harvard Law School

1992 — Barack marries Michelle Robinson

1995 — Barack's memoir, *Dreams from My Father*, is published

1996 — Barack is elected to the Illinois State Senate

1998 — Daughter Malia is born

2001 — Daughter Sasha is born

2005 — Barack is sworn in as the US Senator from Illinois

2006 — Barack's second book, *The Audacity of Hope*, is published

2009 — Barack is sworn in as the 44th president of the USA
Barack is awarded the Nobel Peace Prize

2010 — Barack signs the Affordable Care Act ("Obamacare") into l

2012 — Barack is reelected to serve a second term as president

2017 — Barack leaves office; Donald J. Trump is inaugurated

TIMELINE OF THE WORLD

President John F. Kennedy forms the Peace Corps — **1961**

Martin Luther King, Jr., makes his "I have a dream" — **1963**
speech in Washington, D.C.
President John F. Kennedy is assassinated

Martin Luther King, Jr., is assassinated — **1968**

Apollo 11 lands on the moon — **1969**

President Richard Nixon resigns — **1974**

Saddam Hussein becomes president of Iraq — **1979**

Apple releases its first Macintosh computer — **1984**

Hole in the ozone layer is discovered — **1985**

Space shuttle *Challenger* explodes after lift-off — **1986**

Berlin Wall falls, and Cold War ends — **1989**

Persian Gulf War begins with Iraq's invasion of Kuwait — **1990**

International UFO Museum opens in Roswell, New Mexico — **1992**

Dolly the sheep, the first cloned mammal, is born — **1996**

On September 11, terrorists attack the Twin Towers in — **2001**
New York City and the Pentagon in Washington, D.C.

Iraq War begins — **2003**

Lincoln Bicentennial is celebrated — **2009**
Barbie celebrates her 50th anniversary

Osama bin Laden is killed — **2011**

Hillary R. Clinton becomes the Democratic Party's — **2016**
presidential candidate, the first woman to accomplish this

BIBLIOGRAPHY

Ignatius, Adi., ed. **President Obama: The Path to The White House**. New York: Time Books, 2008.

Obama, Barack. **Dreams From My Father: A Story of Race and Inheritance**. New York: Three Rivers Press, 1996.

Obama, Barack. **The Audacity of Hope**. New York: Crown Publishers, 2006.

*Thomas, Garen. **Yes We Can: A Biography of Barack Obama**. New York: Macmillan, 2008.

*The New York Times, Jill Abramson, and Bill Keller. **Obama: The Historic Journey**. New York: Callaway, 2009.

The starred books are for young readers.